Turn Me Loose

EST. 75 1938
YEARS
THE UNIVERSITY OF GEORGIA PRESS 2013

Turn Me Loose

THE UNGHOSTING OF
MEDGAR EVERS

Poems By
Frank X Walker

The University of
Georgia Press
Athens and London

Published by The University of Georgia Press
Athens, Georgia 30602
www.ugapress.org
© 2013 by Frank X Walker
All rights reserved
Designed by Kaelin Chappell Broaddus
Set in 10/14 Century Old Style
Manufactured by Sheridan Books

The paper in this book meets the guidelines for
permanence and durability of the Committee on
Production Guidelines for Book Longevity of the
Council on Library Resources.

Printed in the United States of America
14 15 16 17 P 5

Library of Congress Cataloging-in-Publication Data

Walker, Frank X., 1961–
[Poems. Selections]
Turn me loose : the unghosting of Medgar Evers :
poems / by Frank X. Walker.
pages cm
Includes bibliographical references.
ISBN-13: 978-0-8203-4541-3 (pbk. : alk. paper)
ISBN-10: 0-8203-4541-5 (pbk. : alk. paper)
1. Evers, Medgar Wiley, 1925–1963–Poetry.
2. United States—Race relations—Poetry. I. Title.
PS3623.A359T87 2013
811'.6–dc23
2012046531

British Library Cataloging-in-Publication Data available

*Dedicated to the
Mississippi Truth Project
and the invisible army
of soldiers for justice
whose names might
never be spoken.*

If I die, it will be in a good cause.
I've been fighting for America just
as much as the soldiers in Vietnam.
I do not believe in violence either by
whites or Negroes. That is why I am
working tirelessly with the NAACP in
a peaceful struggle for justice.

—MEDGAR EVERS

When I go to Hades, I'm going to raise
hell all over Hades till I get to the white
section. For the next 15 years we here
in Mississippi are going to have to do
a lot of shooting to protect our wives
and children from a lot of bad niggers.

—BYRON DE LA BECKWITH

Contents

Foreword

HOW DO WE COMPLY?

ANSWERING THE CALL OF MEDGAR EVERS

Kentucky assumes a prominent place in Frank X Walker's five previous poetry collections. *Affrilachia* (2000) was his first collection and serves as the defining text of black life and experience in the Bluegrass State. *Black Box: Poems* (2006) extends Walker's voice and vision of the overlooked lives of black people in Kentucky through a consideration of his own Affrilachian life. Walker's persona poems keenly focus the issues of racial subjectivity and place through the embodied narratives of black subjects with deep Kentucky ties. *Buffalo Dance: The Journey of York* (2004) and *When Winter Come: The Ascension of York* (2008) imagined what life might have been like for York, the lone black man on the Lewis and Clark expedition. York had been enslaved in Louisville, Kentucky, and served as William Clark's body servant. Walker also eloquently lays to rest Kentucky native Isaac Murphy through a graceful imagining of his inner life and a careful crafting of the lives of his dear ones in *Isaac Murphy: I Dedicate This Ride* (2010). *Turn Me Loose: The Unghosting of Medgar Evers*, Walker's most recent collection, turns toward a deeper South, but not away from the subject of the overlooked lives of black people who make up life there.

By most accounts, Medgar Evers's contributions to the modern day civil rights movement have been overlooked if not forgotten in chronicles of the movement and so from modern memory.[1] These poems masterfully confront this erasure through an engagement with Evers's prominence in the inner workings of white supremacist identity and its manifestation as violence in both formal and informal practices of segregation. This collection underscores the startling incongruity of this contemporary elision given the prominence Evers held as a contestant to the order of white supremacy. To this end, Evers was all but invisible and marginal to assassin Byron De La Beckwith or to the White Citizens Council, the Ku Klux Klan, Governor Ross Barnett, and the Mississippi police. This meant that Evers was also all but invisible as a figure for every black person who dared to challenge formal Jim Crow laws and "Dixie decorum," which Walker's poems identify as those unwritten rules wherein black people publicly acknowledged their inferiority before whites.

Walker beautifully sets in relief the ways that Medgar Evers's singular life symbolizes black life in Mississippi. These poems create an intimate portrait of what it must have been like for people to live amid state-sanctioned loathing; the effort that must have been required to recover dignity from relentless efforts to infuse indignity into the meaningfulness of blackness, from constantly deflecting racist blows. Walker's consideration of the life and cold-blooded assassination of Evers dramatizes the daily horror of dehumanization that thoroughly sought out every corner of southern existence in an effort to degrade the quality of black life and reduce its quantity to prove this point. Indeed, the specter of Evers proves seriousness of purpose in maintaining white supremacy in the segregated South, especially in Mississippi.

Mississippi could create Halloween in August, memorably making a monstrous mask of young Emmett Till's face eight years before Alabama made ghouls of four little Sunday school girls in September. Mississippi muted the voices of its black majority by denying whole counties of black citizens the right to vote, at the same time amplifying the cry of one black woman whose "Mississippi appendectomy" gave involuntary sterilization its name. Mississippi amplified the voice of a governor whose ardent love for segregation ignited the passions of a crowd sympathetic to blocking one black student's admittance into law school at Ole Miss and set the symbolic bar for an Alabama governor's stand in another schoolhouse door.[2]

Walker's poems paint a vivid picture of Mississippi macabre but also of the elegance that black people made of life there. Such elegance gets imagined just as I remember observing it in my own Affrilachian life. I knew and saw black people who could be quiet together; who when alone could think sweetly or soberly about the other; who enjoyed one another with careful measure; who nurtured one another; who not only slept together but rested together. *I believe* the persona that Walker ascribes to Myrlie Evers, who conjures sweet memories when the smooth sound of Motown plays in her ear. *I see* the children she lays down to bed and the dreams she nurtures in a place that insists she does not belong. *I admire* the hope she continues to sustain and the arguments she continues to make for love.

These poems perform. You not only see the drama unfold but you hear the way that Walker scores it. Music can be heard throughout this work. You not only hear it in reading the epigraphs but also through the interpretative acoustics of the surprising fusion of voices throughout. The opening epigraphs featuring the one instance where Medgar Evers speaks set against the voice of Byron De La Beckwith marvelously frame the "divergent points of view" that Walker identifies in his introduction. Having these two men's words together on the same page reflects the stark differences between points of entry and perspectives on living well in Mississippi. Walker offers his work as an "interruption of the silence" concerning Evers's erasure as a civil rights legend and thus serves as an attempt to address an important oversight in a long and terrible legacy of southern violence. This interruption comes to figure reconciliation and possibly healing from the catastrophic wounding that is marked specifically by the assassination of Evers but that also exceeds his ghost. His final words, "turn me loose," were an address to history, but his ghost highlights the liveliness of history. Thus, the title, the epigraphs, and the introduction establish the enormity of this project, which I see as the hard work of reconciliation in light of the nature of the wound and given the absurdity of its situatedness in southern history. Walker brings this point to sonic resonance most profoundly through his thoughtful treatment of "Dixie" and "Strange Fruit."

The section headings "Dixie Suite," "Look Away, Look Away...," "Gallant South," and "Bitter Fruit" reference "Dixie" or "Strange Fruit" respectively. The "Dixie Suite" captures the vast gulf between stark racial impressions of southern life measured by reactions to the song. Amid disputes over the true origin of the song's creation, Mount Vernon, Ohio, native Daniel Decatur Emmett is credited with writing the song.[3] Emmett penned the song as a member of Bryant's Minstrels. "Dixie" assumed its gravity with the onset of the Civil War, when it became the adopted anthem of the Confederacy, and it held its seriousness of purpose when northern and southern bands composed versions of it that were performed throughout the war. While many versions of "Dixie" exist, the voice of the enslaved longing to return to plantation life has endured. Backbreaking and unremitting, unremunerated work gets imagined as tranquil longing through the laboring body of an enslaved person. For those who symbolize those laboring bodies, nostalgia for such a past and pride in this imagined South offends historical recognition of the toll of the historical South upon their lives.

Like jazz artist Rene Marie, "Turn Me Loose" aestheticizes an unlikely entanglement, creating a beautiful ambivalence that invests "Dixie" with new meaning.[4] "Look Away, Look Away..." as a section title brilliantly raises an ethical question regarding bearing witness. It asks: to what extent can looking away align with loyalty? In the final section of "On Collective Memory," Maurice Halbwachs posits that sometimes looking away offers us our only chance at loyalty.[5] He reads Peter's betrayal of Christ as just such a moment. Halbwachs reasonably asserts that when someone we love is about to experience something brutal or horrific, our impulse is not to stare or to be consumed with longing looks; instead, our impulse leads us to look away. Halbwachs contends that from this perspective, Peter had to turn away from Jesus, who was like a brother to him. Thus, in order for Peter to serve as a witness for Christ, he had to deny their brotherhood.

The poems in the section "Look Away, Look Away. . ." imagine the making of Evers into the NAACP field secretary who would become the necessary witness to the "strange and bitter crop" produced in his own backyard. Evers's witness identified his steadfast loyalty to the lives of those who, according to Abel Meeropol, were the by-products of a macabre southern ecology. Under the pen name Lewis Allen, Meeropol wrote a poem, "Bitter Fruit," that would become the lyric of the song "Strange Fruit" in 1939 as an indictment of lynching as a natural feature of the South.[6] In the song, lynching, an extralegal, vigilante practice of killing mostly black people through burning, mutilation, and hanging, serves as an environmental, regional, and racial indictment of a grisly southern tradition made to look like an ecological norm. Where "Dixie" celebrates, "Strange Fruit" indicts.

Though Evers was brutally murdered, much like the victims whose stories he recorded, historian Taylor Branch notes that the killing of Evers was not referred to as a lynching but an assassination. Thus, "the murder of Medgar Evers changed the language of race in American mass culture overnight," according to Branch.[7] Walker acknowledges this difference through the way that he deconstructs the song's text to rethink Evers's legacy. The "Gallant South," taken from the first line of the second stanza of "Strange Fruit" emphasizes various spectacles and spectral scenes that extend the singular startling, grisly one. Through this broadened lens, the scope of violence opens to reveal other, more anesthetized forms of violence usually hidden behind other, more visible forms of brutality. Walker reveals the way that violence looks in dreams; the way it can inform how you imagine love; how it can transform lives and makes for unlikely unions. The voice of Myrlie Evers comes to stand for the living possibility of a "gallant South" as she converts the Willie and Thelma De La Beckwith cabal into a sisterhood in which her life intertwines with theirs.

The final section of *Turn Me Loose*, "Bitter Fruit," cites the original title of the poem that would become "Strange Fruit." Such a return becomes an act of remembrance much like the act necessary to answer the call of Medgar Evers. If we are to finally lay him to rest, to satisfy his request to *turn him loose*, we must remember. This remembrance, however, eschews the wistful recollection of a magnolia-scented South and embraces memories of the flowery scent mixed with the stench of roasting flesh. Compliance requires the recollection of putrescent truths. This remembrance would involve recognizing the on-going presence of the past in the brutal killing of James Craig Anderson. We will have complied with Medgar Evers's request to *turn him loose* when we bring all of our creative powers to bear on questioning the return of the past. Frank X Walker's collection of poems offers a worthy model for how we can deploy the imagination in service to the urgent call of history.

Michelle S. Hite

SPELMAN COLLEGE

NOTES

1. See Manning Marable, "A Servant-Leader of the People: Medgar Wiley Evers (1925–1963)," in *The Autobiography of Medgar Evers: A Hero's Life and Legacy Revealed through His Writings, Letters, and Speeches*, ed. Myrlie Evers-Williams and Manning Marable (New York: Basic Books, 2005); Adam Nossiter, *Of Long Memory: Mississippi and the Murder of Medgar Evers* (Cambridge, Mass.: Da Capo Press, 2002).

2. See Taylor Branch, *Parting the Waters: America in the King Years 1954–63* (New York: Simon & Schuster, 1998); Taylor Branch, *Pillar of Fire: America in the King Years 1963–64* (New York: Touchstone, 1999); John Dittmer, *Local People: The Struggle for Civil Rights in Mississippi* (Urbana: University of Illinois Press, 1995); Chana Kai Lee, *For Freedom's Sake: The Life of Fannie Lou Hamer* (Urbana: University of Illinois Press, 2000); Spike Lee, *4 Little Girls* (HBO Home Video, 2001); Christopher Metress, *The Lynching of Emmett Till: A Documentary Narrative* (Charlottesville: University of Virginia Press, 2002); Dorothy Roberts, *Killing the Black Body: Race, Reproduction, and the Meaning of Liberty (New York: Pantheon Books, 1997)*; Stephen J. Whitfield, *A Death in the Delta: The Story of Emmett Till* (Baltimore: The Johns Hopkins University Press, 1991).

3. See Howard L. Sacks and Judith Rose Sacks, *Way Up North in Dixie: A Black Family's Claim to the Confederate Anthem* (Washington, D.C.: Smithsonian Institution Press, 1993).

4. See René Marie, *Voice of My Beautiful Country* (Motéma, 2011).

5. Maurice Halbwachs, "The Legendary Topography of the Gospels in the Holy Land," part 2 in *On Collective Memory,* trans. and ed. Lewis Coser, (Chicago: University of Chicago Press, 1992).

6. See David Margolick, *Strange Fruit: The Biography of a Song* (New York: The Ecco Press, 2001).

7. Branch, *Pillar of Fire*, 108.

Acknowledgments

Grateful acknowledgment is made to the following publications, in which earlier versions of some of the poems were first published:

The Active Voice: "Last Meal"

Black Magnolia Literary Journal: "After Birth," "Arlington," "Beckwith Dreaming III," "Believing in Hymn," "Evers Family Secret Recipe," "Homecoming," "Southern Girls"

Crab Orchard Review: "Rotten Fruit"

Iron Mountain Review: "Ambivalence over the Confederate Flag," "Fire Proof," "Listening to Music," "Music, Niggers & Jews," "On Moving to California," "Now One Wants to Be President"

Jelly Bucket: "After Birth"

The Louisville Review: "Heavy Wait," "White Knights"

95 Notes Literary Magazine: "Anatomy of Hate"

Obsidian: "Husbandry"

Reverie: "After Dinner in Money, Mississippi"

Weave Magazine: "Swamp Thing," "Harriet Tubman as Villain"

A special thanks to the following for lending their eyes and hearts to early drafts of these poems and especially to those who gifted their brilliant questions, suggestions, and edits toward the final manuscript: Lewis White, Lee Newton, Ama Codjoe, Adam Banks, Debra Kinley, Tammy Ramsey, Jim Minick, CX Dillhunt, Drew Dillhunt,

Taunya Phillips, and Michelle Hite. A special thanks to Randall Horton for his interest and support and to Minrose Gwin for including *Turn Me Loose* among the important literature celebrating and commemorating Evers's legacy in her much-needed work, *Remembering Medgar Evers: Writing the Long Civil Rights Movement*.

Introduction

Much of Mississippi's and the South's past is characterized by increased resistance to white supremacy in the face of overt and subtle racism that resulted in a multitude of crimes. These include crimes against the body, crimes against property, the collusion of public and private institutions in preventing access and opportunity to all people, and conspiracies of silence that continue today. This collection of poems seeks to interrupt that silence and shine a light on the important legacy of a civil rights icon all too often omitted from summaries of the era, by giving voice to a particular chapter in this history from multiple and often divergent points of view.

On June 12, 1963, in Jackson, Mississippi, Medgar Evers, the head of the National Association for the Advancement of Colored People (NAACP) in Mississippi, was shot in the back by Byron De La Beckwith in his own driveway and died soon after being transported to a nearby hospital by neighbors. This was the first in a series of high profile assassinations that would cast a shadow on civil rights activities in America in the early 1960s.

The primary speakers in this narrative are Byron De La Beckwith, Medgar Evers's assassin; Beckwith's wives, Mary Louise (Willie) and Thelma De La Beckwith; Medgar Evers's brother, Charles; Evers's widow, Myrlie Evers; and a sixth voice that works like a Greek chorus. Medgar Evers's voice is silent beyond lifting his final words, "... turn me loose," for the title, but his presence, like a ghost, speaks loudly throughout the poems.

I believe acknowledging and working to fully understand history can create opportunities to better understand racism. I offer these imagined poems in hope that art can help complete the important work we continue to struggle with—the access to economic and social justice that Medgar Evers and so many others died for, and ultimately the healing and reconciliation still needed in America.

PART I

Dixie
Suite

WHAT KILLS ME

Myrlie Evers

When people talk about the movement
as if it started in '64, it erases every
body who vanished on the way home
from work or school and is still listed

as missing. It erases the pile of recovered
bodies—some burnt, shot, dismembered,
some beaten just beyond recognition.
It mutes every unsung voice in Mississippi

that dared to speak up—fully understanding
the consequences. When people talk
about the movement as if it started in '64,
it erases his entire life's work.

It means he lived and died for nothing.
And that's worse than killing him   again.

AMBIGUITY OVER THE CONFEDERATE FLAG

In the old south   *life was full of work*
we would sit on the veranda   *from sunup to sundown*

look out over the horizon at   *nothing but fields of cotton*

the young   *children*
who happily played behind   *tried to pick their own weight*

while their mothers   *by age 13 filled 500 lb sacks*
sang rapturous spirituals   *and lived the blues*

those were good ol' days   *for plantation owners*
not having to use the whip   *sharecropping and extending debt*
was more civilized   *was almost more profitable*

than slavery

ROTTEN FRUIT

Byron De La Beckwith

I.

I fish for pleasure and to relax.
It's the best way
to sort out details of a plan
that needs flawless execution.

Every useful thing I know
I learned sitting in the bottom
of a boat across from my granddaddy
in one of Mississippi's finest

fishing holes. How to
pick out the best   spot. How to
get there early. How to lay
low, be patient   and wait.

II.

Watching your cork disappear
in the water, bob back up and run
is as thrilling as sneaking your hand
up under a pretty girl's skirt.

They all put up a lil' fight, at first
but sooner or later a lucky man
will get his hands on a cat;
a patient man, inside a big wide mouth.

5

There's something about the thought
of a wet body, flapping about
and gasping for breath
that gives me chills, even now.

III.

Sometimes we'd just sit and smoke,
swim in some ice cold beers,
enjoy the sound of no women around
or shoot at ghosts if fish weren't biting.

Sometimes we'd get drunk and argue
for hours about who would win
in a fair fight between his nigger, jack,
and that nigger, joe louis.

IV.

He rode me hard for bragging
about catching the big one,
but I know he bragged even harder
about teaching me how   to fish.

Niggers are proof that
Indians fucked buffalo.

—ANONYMOUS

HUMOR ME

Byron De La Beckwith

I was raised with the word nigger
in my mouth. In this part of the south
it is considered our silver spoon.

It practically lived in every good joke
I heard growing up in Mississippi.
The only other good ones were about sex.

But I've seen bad jokes about niggers and sex
kick all the power of whiskey right off
the front porch, turn it into something so mean,

somebody would have to get smacked around
to stir that power back up again. Sometimes
it was a dog too friendly for drunks.

Sometimes it was a girlfriend or a wife
who wandered grinning into our man-talk
and snickered at all the wrong parts.

If there weren't no women or dogs around,
us men would pile into a truck and ride off towards
the coon side of town, looking for something funny.

You can never turn that word
around and make it cool....
It's not a word of love.

—CHUCK D

THE N-WORD

Charles Evers

Hearing that word launched
from the back of any throat

brings back the smell
of German shepherd breath

of fresh gasoline
and sulfur air

of fear—both ours and theirs.

I hear nine brave children
walking a gauntlet of hate in Little Rock

and four innocent little girls
lifted up to heaven too soon.

Instead of a rebel yell
I hear a rifle bark.

Instead of a whiskey-soaked yee haw
I hear a window break

and children sobbing for a father
face down in a pool of blood.

I hear all my faith collapse
on the wings of a woman's scream.

I can't hear anything less
and absolutely nothing   funny.

Pastoral scene of the gallant south . . .

—ABEL MEEROPOL,
  "Strange Fruit," sung by
  Billie Holiday

SOUTHERN SPORTS

Byron De La Beckwith

Sometimes it starts with a bonfire
or begins with taunting and spitting

quickly graduating to cursing
and punching and kicking

some body   as hard as you can
for the sheer joy of causing them pain

as entertainment for the crowd now
celebrating the crack or pop of broken bodies

showering outstanding individual
violence with applause and cheers.

All you need is some body wearing
the color you've been taught to hate

some body threatening to take
what's rightfully yours

and a little girl with her thighs exposed
held high in the air and screaming.

BYRON DE LA BECKWITH
DREAMING I

Mamma's holding a baby
with perfect blue eyes

she drops it when a tea kettle
screams

she reaches for me
but I start to float away

there is a sound like a loud
hand clap and suddenly

I'm floating face up
in a thick warm soup

the air smells like our bathroom
when Willie's on the rag

I drink down all the soup and a crowd
gathers around me singing "Dixie"

I'D WISH I WAS IN DIXIE TOO

If your family's wealth depended on those
you enslaved and the cotton they spun into gold;

if your intellectual superiority depended on
hundreds of years of denying literacy to others

while your color confirmed your right to do so;
if the thought of being responsible for your own

hoeing, planting, chopping, picking, smithing,
raking, mucking, shoeing, milking, smoking,

canning, baking, hauling, cooking, serving,
sweeping, washing, ironing, fixing, nursing,

mending, dusting, and cleaning makes you tired;
then I understand why you love that song so much.

PART II

Southern Dreams

FIRE PROOF

Willie De La Beckwith

He would come home
from evening rallies and secret meetings
so in love with me

I could never see nothing wrong
with what he did with his hands.
I just pretended I didn't know

what gunpowder smelled like
or why he kept his rifles so clean.
If he walked through that door

and said, "Willie, burn these clothes,"
I'd pile them on the coals and stare
at the fire. I'd listen to the music

twix the crackle and calm as we danced.
And while the ashes gathered 'round
their own kind in the bottom of the grate

I'd watch the embers glow like our bedroom did.
Now, I ain't saying he was right or wrong.
He often confused hatred with desire.

But if you ain't never set a man on fire,
felt him explode inside you then die in your arms,
honey, you got no idea what I'm talking about.

It was a touch. It was a look . . .
It was music playing.

—MYRLIE EVERS

LISTENING TO MUSIC

The right song slow dancing through the air
at the end of a long day full of kids

and no husband, could not only set the tone,
but put the sound of yesterday back in the air.

Smokey Robinson and the Miracles crooned
all the sweet words that his eyes whispered

across the doorframe when he finally came home,
but more often than not, it was Sam Cooke

and Ray Charles or Bobby Blue Bland taking turns
in my ears, reminding me how much I loved that man

no matter how mad or lonely I might have felt.
The right song was like a Kodak Brownie of us cuddling

or an atlas mapping out all our rough spots
and the ways around them. After sweet talking him out

of his suit and tie, after he unloaded the day's burdens,
we melted together in the dark, beneath the covers

and the crackle of the radio. The sound of my guys
singing backup and Medgar's jack hammer heart

finally slowing to match our leaky faucet, as he fell asleep
in my arms, completing the soundtrack for a perfect night.

LIFE APES ART APES LIFE: BYRON DE LA BECKWITH REFLECTS ON *BIRTH OF A NATION*

I was told that the president of these United States
said that film was *truth written in lightning*

25,000 proud hooded knights marched
through Atlanta just to celebrate the opening.

What an electric moment it must have been
sitting in a whites only theater

being right there in the balcony, beside Booth
when that pretty little bullet kissed Lincoln on the head

laughing out loud at clown nigger politicians
pretending to run meetings and pass laws

wiping their asses on the Constitution
pissing on the South and calling it reconstruction

How hard it must have been to sit on your hands
and not shoot at the moving pictures when the actors

made up like coons chased after white women.
I can almost hear the crowd whoop and shout

when the heroes thundered into town at the end,
white robes, hoods and guns gleaming in the sun

dispensing an Old Testament justice on the screen
as clear as Revelations for Christian men like me.

WHITE OF WAY

after A. Van Jordan

Byron De La Beckwith

[White] **Power,** *noun*
1 belief in the fact that all white people have the God given and constitutionally guaranteed right to exercise, encourage, promote, celebrate and defend the privilege of being born superior to other races.

[White] **Pride,** *noun*
1 a feeling of deep pleasure or satisfaction derived from the knowledge that *all* members of other races possess behaviors or abilities that distinguish them as inferior with the obvious exception of athletes, musicians, and comedians like *Amos and Andy* who make white folks laugh so hard they damn near piss themselves. The same goes for the tap dancing nigger butler on the *Shirley Temple Show*, and that nigger *Uncle Ben* on the rice box. They're all always shuffling and bent over with big ol' dickless grins on their faces. They're the only niggers a white man could ever trust with his daughters.

[White] **Privilege,** see *Colonialism, Apartheid,
and Manifest Destiny.*

Synonyms: Patriot, Religious Right, Conservative Christian, Staunch Segregationist, proud American, active Klansman, card carrying member of the Citizens Council, Mississippi Sovereignty Commission, Redeemers; commonly confused with *racist, xenophobe,* or *bigot.*

MUSIC, NIGGERS & JEWS

Byron De La Beckwith

Long before George Jones and others
had folks all over the country hungry

for a weekly plate of Hee Haw
and the Grand Ole Opry, TV pretended

regular, hardworking, blue collar,
proud-to-be-white folks, didn't exist.

Johnny Cash went on Carson in '64
and damn near set the stage on fire.

His songs was real music—not none
of that monkey shine they tried to sell

with white faces on the cover.
But as good as Johnny was and is,

American Bandstand, Rock 'n Roll,
and them long-haired sissies from England

made living rooms full of our young
almost apologize for being born white.

Dick Clark is no better than a nigger to me
and the Jews that control television is even less.

SWAMP THING

Willie De La Beckwith

My ears were field with cotton.
My throat had been lynched shut.

I was chained to something as big
and long and dark as Mississippi herself.

Magnolia trees were bleeding. The floor
was turning to marsh beneath my feet.

I called out for help, but only laughter
and spit came out of my whip.

When I felt the cold metal hounds
biting my ankles, I sat up in bed,

screaming and chasing my breath,

only to find my husband
grinning and tickling my feet.

STAND BY YOUR MAN

Willie De La Beckwith

Like any smart woman
I've stormed out

even divorced him once
to make my point

but anybody
who even stops

takes time
to think about it

and still makes
their lips ask why

I'm so proud to be
Mrs. Byron De La Beckwith

ain't never heard
Tammy Wynnette sing

—and she's
from Mississippi too.

HUSBANDRY

Myrlie Evers

I fell in love with his desire to take his fear
make Mississippi something stronger out of it.

Put my plans on hold to breathe him up close
help him plant his dreams for a better South.

Wove my spine to his so he could stand
magnolia tall and blossom for all to see.

Birthed him namesakes with enough arms
to carry all of his tomorrows.

He spent every penny of his strength organizing
for a hate-free day and we didn't waste a single night.

UNWRITTEN RULES FOR YOUNG BLACK BOYS WANTING TO LIVE IN MISSISSIPPI LONG ENOUGH TO BECOME MEN

Rule number one. White is always right.

Number two. Never look a white man in the eye.

Three. Always answer *yes Sir* or *no Ma'am*
    when spoken to by whites.

Four. Always look for, use or request the colored section.

Five. Never speak to, smile at or stare in the direction
    of a white woman.

Six. Pretend your name really is boy, son, or worse.

Seven. Ignore all white sexual aggression
    towards your sisters, mothers, or aunts.

Eight. Always suppress your anger, cynicism, and rage
    or mask it with a wide grin, pretend stupidity, and silence.

Nine. If a white man says it looks like rain, wish out loud
    for an umbrella no matter how dry it is.

Ten. If you forget any of these rules, fall back on rule number one.

PART IIII

Look Away,
Look Away...

BYRON DE LA BECKWITH
DREAMING II

I am driving a new white Cadillac
but instead of gunning it and kicking up red dirt

I'm joy riding Sunday-slow on a country road
of wooly black heads

I slam on the breaks
and suddenly I can hear them breathing,

when I floor the pedal they start to sing
and the faster I drive the louder they howl

my steering wheel and windshield disappear
the leather seats turn to pine

the caddy rolls right into a church
where somebody is beating

the hell out of a tambourine
and it gets louder and louder and louder

until my woman screams
and we both look down

to see she has given birth
to what we first thought

was a mongrel baby
but after I throw it in the Mississippi

I can see it was just covered with blood.

AFTER DINNER
IN MONEY, MISSISSIPPI

after Tyehimba Jess

pick up

a tool and beat   any nigger looking at

white eggs   white women

white sugar   or anything white but cotton

wait until after

dark

corn syrup, vanilla

extract

a confession at gun point

salt

open wounds

and butter

pour into

a thin crust   the Tallahatchie River

cover

with pecans   up the truth

bake   with a 75-lb

cotton gin fan

let things cool

ready when brown and puffy

WORLD WAR TOO

Myrlie Evers

Medgar, Charles, and men like them
survived Jim Crow Army,
the Blitzkrieg, and Messerschmitts.

They returned home and fought
for a Double Victory
against the axis powers
of poll taxes, literacy tests, and violence.

The battle now was to have some say
in their own lives.

I once was blind, but thank God I
can see
It was because grace and mercy
came along and rescued me.

—MISSISSIPPI MASS CHOIR

BELIEVING IN HYMN

Myrlie Evers

Whenever we needed more confidence
than we woke up with in the morning

God would come in a song
wearing a black woman's voice

a voice that sounded like that far away
look in Reverend Martin Luther King's eyes.

When she opened it up, it wrapped its arms
around all our fears, our doubts;

it lifted our hearts and spirits and took up
so much space there was no room to hate back.

Every time she laid down a verse over the roar
of fire hoses, attack dogs, and police batons,

our own voices would join hands, pick it up
and let the chorus carry us as far as we needed to go.

white men would say they were
going out to the quarters to
have their luck changed.

—ANONYMOUS

SOUTHERN BELLS

Willie De La Beckwith

When our grandfathers strutted back
from the slave quarters
still unzipped and whiskey-eyed

and on occasion forgetting
it was a sweet southern belle
they were now wringing

when the mongrel evidence of their sins
crowded the edge of the front porch
or tiptoed around our kitchens

with swollen bellies—thus began
our great tradition
of not knowing and not wanting to know

of never ever asking about
what happened
out there   in the dark

but, if you really know a man
you know what he loves
and you know what ignites his lust

whether that be the peal and chime
of a black woman's body
or the silent one   of her man.

FIGHTING EXTINCTION

Byron De La Beckwith

We do what we do to build a fort around our women
and to protect America from mongrelization.

Allowing the free mixing of colored and white
is worse than too much pepper on a bowl of grits.

Have you not seen what one drop of black
paint will do to a gallon of white?

I ain't afraid of niggers, but I have nightmares
about the end of whiteness

and waking up one morning, pulling back the sheet
only to find my Willie is Aunt Jemima.

HARRIET TUBMAN AS VILLAIN:
A GHOST STORY

Willie De La Beckwith

There was a scary ol' black woman ghost
that carried a shotgun and snuck into the quarters
at night to steal little picaninnies an' field hands.

She carried each one of 'em down to the creek
and covered 'em with mud to hide their scent,
then sang a magic song that made 'em all invisible.

They ran away so quickly even the bloodhounds
couldn't catch 'em. She came back night after night
until she'd stole nearly every nigger in the quarters

and come spring there was hardly anybody to break
the ground and drop the seeds. In the summer
there was almost nobody to chop the cotton

when harvest time come, the poor old farmer and his wife
picked what they'd planted by themselves, worked
every day 'til sundown and even took supper in the fields.

They were both found on Christmas day, bent over
and frozen to a cotton bush, fingers and hands cut up
and still bleeding, after working themselves   to death.

LEGAL LYNCHING

The registration of Negro voters
and demonstrations for civil rights
is strictly prohibited.

Violators will be punished
with racial epithets, harassing
phone calls, rocks, and eggs

(thrown from cars and trucks)
and firebombs when necessary.
Repeat offenders run the risk

of being immediately separated
from places of employment
and having mortgages called in.

Organizers of said activities
will be dealt with harshly
outside the highest limits of the law.

AFTER THE FBI
SEARCHED THE BAYOU

Myrlie Evers

When they unearthed
each new corpse,
we couldn't speak for days.

We came back
from that dark place
in tears—not for ourselves,

but for all the mutilated
and charred remains that were not
Goodman, Schwerner, or Chaney.

We could only find solace
looking out over the Mississippi,
watching that dark woman

swallow   the sun.

HAIKU FOR EMMETT TILL

Up north, nobody thought
it necessary to teach
Dixie decorum

Did he whistle or
flirt, forget the Negro's place?
Was it eyeball rape?

The all-white jury
guzzled beer, while his mamma
shed tears on the stand

They looked at his skull
his disfigured face, smiled, and
still voted not guilty

Fourteen is too soon
to visit Mississippi
come home   in a box

NO MORE FEAR

Myrlie Evers

Three months before Emmett Till arrived
Reverend George Lee was killed
by a shotgun blast to the face.

It was ruled a traffic accident.

He had been the first to register
to vote in his county.

One week before Emmett Till arrived
Lamar Smith voted in the democratic primary
and was shot at high noon
in front of the county courthouse.

There were no arrests.

Medgar cried when he heard about young Till.
Then he dressed as a sharecropper
helped find witnesses
and smuggled them out of town
for their safety.

When Uncle Mose stood up in court,
pointed right at J. W. Milam, identified him
as the killer, we thought the air would split,
but it didn't.

Instead a seam opened up in that place
where we kept all our fears.

WHEN DEATH MOVED IN

Myrlie Evers

It attached itself to our lives, first
like an unplanned pregnancy,

then like our fourth child.
We didn't talk about its disfigured face

or its crooked limbs and spine.
We went about the people's business

tried to pretend that it wasn't really there,
though some nights it filled every open space

in the room, often crawling into bed between us,
making it difficult to sleep.

Every new registered voter, successful boycott,
demonstration and prime-time television minute

put fat on its face. Images of Medgar
escorting James Meredith into Ole Miss

were celebrated with new front teeth.
When it crawled to the front door, and spoke

its first cuss words
it sounded like a car backfired   twice.

PART IV

Gallant
South

BYRON DE LA BECKWITH
DREAMING III

I unzip my pants to piss,
and my fingers pull out a long black snake.

Willie reaches over, strokes it,
and smiles. I squeeze my eyes shut,

clear my head, enjoy the weight of it
in my hands, open my right eye to a squint,

line up the crosshairs,
take a deep breath   and smile back.

AFTER BIRTH

Like them, a man can conceive
an idea, an event, a moment so clearly
he can name it   even before it breathes.

We both can carry a thing around inside
for only so long and no matter how small
it starts out, it can swell and get so heavy

our backs hurt and we can't find comfort
enough to sleep at night. All we can think
about is the relief that waits, at the end.

When it was finally time, it was painless.
It was the most natural thing I'd ever done.
I just closed my eyes and squeezed

then opened them and there he was,
just laying there still covered with blood,
(laughs) but already trying to crawl.

I must admit, like any proud parent
I was afraid at first, afraid he'd live,
afraid he'd die too soon.

Funny how life 'n death
is a whole lot of pushing and pulling,
holding and seeking breath;

a whole world turned upside down
until   some   body   screams.

44

SORORITY MEETING

Myrlie Evers speaks to Willie
and Thelma De La Beckwith

My faith urges me to love you.
My stomach begs me to not.
All I know is that day
made us sisters, somehow. After long
nervous nights and trials on end
we are bound together

in this unholy sorority of misery.
I think about you every time I run
my hands across the echoes
in the hollows of my sheets.
They seem loudest just before I wake.
I open my eyes every morning

half expecting Medgar to be there,
then I think about you
and your eyes always snatch me back.
Your eyes won't let me forget.

We are sorority sisters now
with a gut-wrenching country ballad
for a sweetheart song, tired funeral
and courtroom clothes for colors
and secrets we will take to our graves.

I was forced to sleep night after night
after night with a ghost.
You chose to sleep   with a killer.

We all pledged our love,
crossed our hearts and swallowed oaths
before being initiated   with a bullet.

ONE-THIRD OF
180 GRAMS OF LEAD

Both of them were history, even before one
pulled the trigger, before I rocketed through
the smoking barrel hidden in the honeysuckle
before I tore through a man's back, shattered

his family, a window, and tore through an inner wall
before I bounced off a refrigerator and a coffeepot
before I landed at my destined point in history
—next to a watermelon. What was cruel was the irony

not the melon, not the man falling in slow motion,
but the man squinting through the crosshairs
reducing the justice system to a small circle, praying
that he not miss, then sending me to deliver a message

as if the woman screaming in the dark
or the children crying at her feet
could ever believe
a bullet   was small enough   to hate.

ARLINGTON

Myrlie Evers

During the flag ceremony
soldiers folded, creased, tucked,
smoothed, and then folded again

with such precision and care,
I imagined they were wrapping
a body

a red, white, and blue
mummy
which they passed, and saluted

and honored so much so
everybody stopped looking
at the casket

by the time they placed that triangle
of husband in my arms,
they left no doubt

I was holding his future
and what we were burying
was only his past.

CROSS-EXAMINATION

Byron De La Beckwith

What good would it do to own a whole orchard
and not make preserves out of the fruit?

Any fool with money and a passion for guns
is at most, a collector. Only a marksman like me

could truly own a rifle like that or any gun.
Owning a gun is like driving a fast car.

Hell, it's like raising prize cocks. You gotta keep
'em healthy and mean. You gotta let 'em out

of they cage sometimes and rev the engines
just to see 'em strut. Now, I ain't saying I did it,

that's for the state to prove, but you gotta be a fool
to own a car and not know how fast it'll go.

And whatever I am, I ain't no fool.

BIGHEARTED

Thelma De La Beckwith speaks to Myrlie Evers

You are wrong to think my man a monster
or a lowly coward 'cause he grins at you

from across the courtroom. Your shallow
Faith won't let you see his generosity

or his compassion. Don't you see the courtesy
he extended to you by opening up a hole

in that boy's black back and not his face,
allowing you and your children the dignity

of an open casket, a vision of perfect sleep
instead of a bloody stump, where his head rests now?

ANATOMY OF HATE

Byron De La Beckwith

I have no problem with colored who know
their place, but it's easy to hate troublemakers

an' integrationists, uppity monkeys in suits'n ties,
little more than pet dogs for northern scum

pissing on our proud Heritage. Yeah, I shot that boy
in the back. But not 'cause I hated his color.

I hated how clean he kept his car. I hated
his always-pressed clothes and shiny shoes. I hated

that he parked in front of his own house. I hated

the sound of the north and schools and books
every time he opened his nigger lips.

The prosecution said he was only speaking
on equality and freedom, but what I heard

when he flapped his black gums was
"poor white trash, lick our union boots

and watch us do to your wives and daughters
what the slavers done to ours."

. . . everybody knows about
Mississippi Goddam.

—NINA SIMONE

WHAT THEY CALL IRONY

Byron De La Beckwith

There was a time
when being a white man
on trial in Mississippi
was like swapping lies
in the barbershop or at a church picnic.

Looking across at the Judases
that helped find me guilty
the third time
was like looking at a souvenir postcard
of a lynching

only it's me playing jump rope
with the tree
and the Christmas morning faces
in the crowd
is all carpetbaggers and Jews.

ON MOVING TO CALIFORNIA

Myrlie Evers

Dying can't compare with living
with death and loss   grief and anger.

Standing up for truth and justice
is much harder than marrying silence.

Climbing out from under the heaviness
of hate is the hardest thing I've ever done.

Surviving a husband is something I prepared for.
I practiced and practiced being strong enough.

Surviving Mississippi took Fannie Lou Hamer
strength, something I didn't ever think I had.

PART V

Bitter
Fruit

ONE MISSISSIPPI,
TWO MISSISSIPPIS

after Thomas Sayers Ellis

You got old plantations
     We got shotgun houses
You got sprawling verandas
     We got a piece a front porch
You got beautiful gardens
     We got cotton fields
You got Ole Miss Law School
     We got Parchman Prison
You got Gulf Shore beaches
     We got river banks
You got debutante balls
     We got juke joints
You got bridge parties
     We got dominoes and spades
You got mint juleps
     We got homemade hooch
You got your grandmother's china
     We got paper plates
You see a proud history
     We see a racist past
You don't remember lynchings
     We can't forget
You got blacks
     We got   the blues

A FINAL ACCOUNTING

You can own the land a woman calls home
but not the warmth in it or the stars above it.

You can own the food she feeds her family
but not the love that prepares it.

You can own the well from which she pulls
her water but not the thirst it quenches

You can fill all the libraries with your version
of facts, call it history, and still not own the truth.

NOW ONE WANTS TO BE PRESIDENT

Thelma De La Beckwith

After that first harvest,
they took to the streets
and chanted "after" *him*
there'd be *no more fear*

but it took them forty-five years
to grow back their spines
after their so-called civil rights lions
were slaughtered like lambs

I look at this new one standing here
shameless and shiny, faking humility
and confidence, an educated mongrel
peddling false hope

But even though he won, the victory is ours,
because it took them forty-five years
to rebuild their backbones

all those years to unshackle their fear

forty-five years to raise another *boy*
man enough to send home   in a box

Plenty of rich folks wants to fight.
Give them the guns.

—WOODY GUTHRIE

EPIPHANY

Willie De La Beckwith

I never understood colored folks.
They ain't got no more than we got.
Hell, most of them got less than nothing
but every time I see one, they are smiling

I don't hate them as much as I hate
those big ass grins on their face.
When I see one of them grinning, it's like
they are laughing at us for being white

and still poor, for believing we had something
in common with the real bosses.
We stood by while the rich used blacks
like they were little more than dirt floors

to walk on, but we were too dumb to know
we were just their rugs.

LAST MEAL HAIKU

Myrlie Evers

imagine byron
sitting down to eat, using
his cotton shirt sleeves

as substitutes for
napkins, clutching a steak knife
—no unleavened bread

enjoying blood that
drips from every single bite
of his final meal

imagine before
he lays down to sleep, ready
to meet his maker

he gets on his knees
and confesses all his sins
in time to be saved,

but when he looks up
at God's burnt brass face he thinks
he has gone   to hell

WHITE KNIGHTS

Myrlie Evers

For every ten Beckwiths
defending the right to wave
the Confederate flag
there's at least one Kennedy.

For every racist governor
and flaming cross
there's a white Catholic priest
dodging bricks, wiping off spit,
bleeding from the temple
in the thick of a march.

For every hundred southerners
teeming with hatred
there's a set of kind blue eyes
full of hope, there's a young heart

unafraid of change and a reason
not to fear or pity them all.

EVERS FAMILY SECRET RECIPE

Myrlie Evers

prepare closed minds
with patience. peel ripe
distrust with smiles.

stir in generous portions
of kindness and willingness
to do the work.

add commitment and determination.
massage out doubt and fear.

blend in a drop of daddy's blood
and two of mamma's tears.

season with hope and change.
let sit for a generation.

distill as a salve. rub deeply into
your children's hands, feet and hearts.

now vote.

THE ASSURANCE MAN

Charles Evers

If you knew him after Alcorn and the war,
before history books, before that bullet,

before becoming the field secretary,
back when he was just an insurance man,

you would've known how bullheaded he could be.
He knew Mississippi polished and perfected ugly

but also that she had something beautiful to offer
her sons   our freedom.

He didn't sell us a waiting game like a preacher
and only promise our rewards in the hereafter.

—GUY AND CANDY CARAWAN

GIFT OF TIME

Myrlie Evers

When I was able to see beauty in a world
littered with scars

when I discovered stores of memories
that a bullet couldn't quit

when I watched a son grow into his father's face,
his laugh, his walk

I saw how faith could be restored.

And was finally able to imagine
that before he fell in love with guns

before he lost his mother
and his childhood

before he needed a reason to hate
to feel threatened

to push back against imaginary walls
collapsing in on him

like August heat and no fan

I imagine before all that, little Byron was good.
He was clean. He was innocent.

And I finally understood
that trouble don't last always.

HEAVY WAIT

If Mississippi is to love her elephant self
she needs a memory as sharp as her ivory tusks
with as many wrinkles as her thick thick past.

If she forgets, she need only reach back,
caress her keloid skin, and run her fingers across
the Braille history raised on her spine
or the bruised couplets around her supple neck.

For Mississippi to love her elephant self,
she need only open her blue/gray eyes and move.

Move, as if she carries the entire weight of history
and southern guilt on her massive head.

Move, in any direction, as long as it is forward.

For Mississippi to love her elephant self,
she must ask for, extend, and receive
forgiveness.

But she must never ever ever   forget.

Time Line

1954   The Supreme Court rules on *Brown v. Board of Education of Topeka Kansas*, unanimously agreeing that segregation in public schools is unconstitutional, paving the way for large-scale desegregation.

1955   Fourteen-year-old Chicagoan Emmett Till, visiting family in Mississippi, is kidnapped, brutally beaten, shot, and dumped in the Tallahatchie River for allegedly whistling at a white woman. The two white men acquitted by an all-white jury later brag about committing the murder in *Look* magazine.

1955   NAACP member Rosa Parks refuses to give up her seat at the front of the "colored section" bus to a white passenger. In response to her arrest, the Montgomery, Alabama, black community launches a successful bus boycott, which will last for more than a year.

1957   Federal troops are sent in to facilitate the integration of formerly all-white Little Rock, Arkansas, Central High School by "the Little Rock Nine."

1962   James Meredith becomes the first black student to enroll at the University of Mississippi. Violence and riots surrounding his enrollment cause President John F. Kennedy to send five thousand federal troops to restore and maintain order.

1963   Byron De La Beckwith shoots Medgar Evers. He is tried twice in 1964 for murder. Both trials result in hung juries. Beckwith goes free.

March on Washington draws over 200,000 people. Martin Luther King, Jr., delivers famous "I Have a Dream" speech.

Four young girls (Denise McNair, Cynthia Wesley, Carole Robertson, and Addie Mae Collins) are killed when a bomb explodes at the Sixteenth Street Baptist Church in Birmingham, Alabama.

President John F. Kennedy assassinated. Warren Commission concludes Lee Harvey Oswald, acting alone, committed the crime.

1964 President Lyndon B. Johnson signs the Civil Rights Act of 1964, which prohibits discrimination of all kinds based on race, color, religion, or national origin.

The bodies of three civil rights workers (James Chaney, Andrew Goodman, & Michael Schwerner)–two white, one black–are found in an earthen dam six weeks after being murdered by the Ku Klux Klan.

1965 Malcolm X is assassinated in the Audubon Ballroom in Harlem.

Blacks begin a march to Montgomery from Selma, Alabama, but are stopped by police at the Pettus Bridge. Fifty marchers are hospitalized after police use tear gas, whips, and clubs against them, earning the incident the name "Bloody Sunday."

Voting Rights Act of 1965 makes it easier for southern blacks to register to vote by outlawing literacy tests, poll taxes, and other such requirements that were instituted to restrict blacks from voting.

Routine traffic stop ignites six-day race riot in Los Angeles, California.

1968 Martin Luther King, Jr., is shot in Memphis, Tennessee, sparking riots in over sixty cities. James Earl Ray is convicted of his murder.

Robert F. Kennedy is assassinated in Los Angeles, California, by Sirhan Sirhan.

1969 Black Panther Party deputy chairman, Fred Hampton, is assassinated as he lies in bed by Chicago Police, FBI, and a tactical unit of the Illinois state attorney's office.

1992   Race riots erupt in south-central Los Angeles after a jury acquits
        four police officers for the videotaped beating of Rodney King.

1994   Thirty years after assassinating Medgar Evers, Byron De La
        Beckwith is convicted for murder at a third trial.

1998   James Byrd, Jr., is murdered by three white supremacists in Jasper,
        Texas, who drag him behind a pickup truck.

2001   Racial tensions ignited by fifteenth shooting death of a young black
        man by police in six years results in riots in Cincinnati, Ohio.

2005   Edgar Ray Killen is convicted of manslaughter forty-one years
        after the deaths of civil rights workers Chaney, Goodman, and
        Schwerner.

2007   Six black students at Jena High School in Central Louisiana are
        arrested and charged with attempted murder after the beating of a
        white classmate.

2008   Barack Obama becomes first African American elected as
        president of the United States.

2011   White teenagers brutally beat, run over, and kill James Anderson
        in Jackson, Mississippi.

2012   Neighborhood watch volunteer shoots and kills unarmed teenager
        Trayvon Martin in Sanford, Florida.

Bibliography

The epigraph in "Humor Me" is taken from the poem "The Social Order," by Andrew Hudgins, in *The Glass Hammer*.

Carson, Clayborne. *Civil Rights Chronicle: The African-American Struggle for Freedom*. Lincolnwood, Ill.: Legacy, 2003.

Delaughter, Bobby. *Never Too Late: A Prosecutor's Story of Justice in the Medgar Evers Case*. Scribner: New York, 2001.

Evers, Myrlie. *For Us, the Living*. Jackson, Miss.: Banner Books, 1967.

Gwin, Minrose. *Remembering Medgar Evers: Writing the Long Civil Rights Movement*. Athens: University of Georgia Press, 2013.

Hampton, Henry and Steve Fayer. *Voices of Freedom: Oral History of the Civil Rights Movement from the 1950s through the 1980s*. New York: Bantam Books, 1990.

Hudgins, Andrew. *The Glass Hammer*. Boston: Houghton Mifflin, 1994.

Massengill, Reed. *Portrait of a Racist: The Real Life of Byron De La Beckwith*. New York: St. Martin's Griffin, 1994.

Mills, Kay. *This Little Light of Mine: The Life of Fannie Lou Hamer*. Lexington: University Press of Kentucky, 2007.

Nossiter, Adam. *Of Long Memory: Mississippi and the Murder of Medgar Evers*. Cambridge, Mass.: Da Capo Press, 1994.

Sims, Patsy. *The Klan*, 2nd ed. Lexington: University Press of Kentucky, 1996.